WILD AND WOOLLY MAMMOTHS

Thousands of years ago, herds of mammoths roamed the earth. They were huge beasts like elephants, with great curving tusks. Some of them lived in icy northern lands, others browsed in deep tropical forests. Hunters trapped them in pits, or killed them with stone-tipped spears. They ate the mammoth meat and used the mammoth bones for everything from tent frames to musical instruments. They painted pictures of mammoths on the walls of their caves.

Aliki, too, has captured the mammoth, in engaging words and pictures. She describes how one whole frozen mammoth was discovered, preserved for centuries in a Siberian glacier. Her book is an appealing account of what scientists have learned about the mammoth's life and the ways of the mammoth hunters.

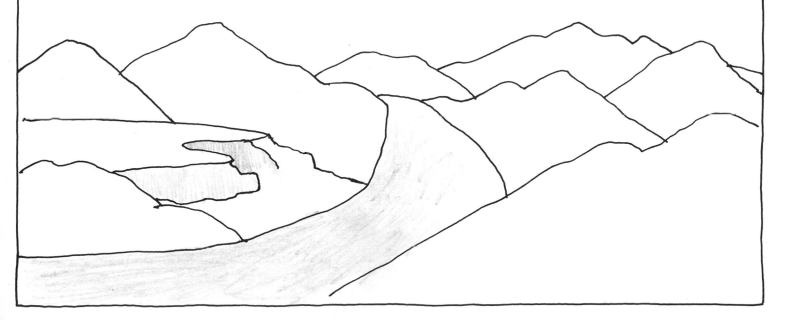

for Flo Stone

WILD AND WOOLLY MAMMOTHS

written and illustrated by

ALIKI, pseud.

Thomas Y. Crowell Company • New York

LET'S-READ-AND-FIND-OUT SCIENCE BOOKS

Editors: **DR. ROMA GANS**, Professor Emeritus of Childhood Education, Teachers College, Columbia University
DR. FRANKLYN M. BRANLEY, Astronomer Emeritus and former Chairman of The American Museum–Hayden Planetarium

LIVING THINGS: PLANTS

Corn Is Maize: The Gift of the Indians
Down Come the Leaves
How a Seed Grows
Mushrooms and Molds
Plants in Winter
Roots Are Food Finders
Seeds by Wind and Water
The Sunlit Sea
A Tree Is a Plant
Water Plants
Where Does Your Garden Grow?

LIVING THINGS: ANIMALS, BIRDS, FISH, INSECTS, ETC.

Animals in Winter
Bats in the Dark
Bees and Beelines
Big Tracks, Little Tracks
Birds at Night
Birds Eat and Eat and Eat
Bird Talk
The Blue Whale
Camels: Ships of the Desert
Cockroaches: Here, There, and Everywhere
Corals

Ducks Don't Get Wet
The Eels' Strange Journey
The Emperor Penguins
Fireflies in the Night
Giraffes at Home
Green Grass and White Milk
Green Turtle Mysteries
Hummingbirds in the Garden
Hungry Sharks
It's Nesting Time
Ladybug, Ladybug, Fly Away Home
Little Dinosaurs and Early Birds
The Long-Lost Coelacanth and Other Living Fossils
The March of the Lemmings
My Daddy Longlegs
My Visit to the Dinosaurs
Opossum
Sandpipers
Shells Are Skeletons
Shrimps
Spider Silk
Spring Peepers
Starfish
Twist, Wiggle, and Squirm: A Book About Earthworms
Watch Honeybees with Me
What I Like About Toads

Why Frogs Are Wet
Wild and Woolly Mammoths

THE HUMAN BODY

A Baby Starts to Grow
Before You Were a Baby
A Drop of Blood
Fat and Skinny
Find Out by Touching
Follow Your Nose
Hear Your Heart
How Many Teeth?
How You Talk
In the Night
Look at Your Eyes*
My Five Senses
My Hands
The Skeleton Inside You
Sleep Is for Everyone
Straight Hair, Curly Hair*
Use Your Brain
What Happens to a Hamburger
Your Skin and Mine*

And other books on AIR, WATER, AND WEATHER; THE EARTH AND ITS COMPOSITION; ASTRONOMY AND SPACE; and MATTER AND ENERGY

* Available in Spanish

Library of Congress Cataloging in Publication Data Aliki. Wild and woolly mammoths. (Let's-read-and-find-out science books)
SUMMARY: An easy-to-read account of the woolly mammoth, a giant land mammal which has been extinct for over 11,000 years.
1. Mammoth—Juv. lit. [1. Mammoth] I. Title. QE882.P8A43 1977 569'.6 76-18082 ISBN 0-690-01276-4 (lib. bdg.)

10 9 8 7 6 5 4 3 2 1

WILD AND WOOLLY MAMMOTHS

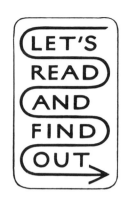

LET'S READ AND FIND OUT

Thousands of years ago, a wild and woolly beast
   roamed the northern part of the earth.
It had two great, curved tusks
   and a long, hairy trunk.
Its big bones were covered with tough skin
   and soft fur.
The long hair on its humped back reached
   almost to the ground.
It looked like an elephant, but it was not quite as
   big.
It was a woolly mammoth.

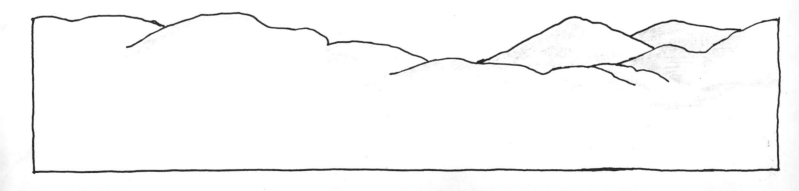

Hundreds of woolly mammoths lived during the
   last Ice Age.
Long before then, the earth was hot and swampy.
That was when the dinosaurs lived.

Slowly, the earth grew cold.
Some places in the north were so cold
    the snow never melted.
It formed into great rivers of ice called glaciers.

Many animals died out because of the cold.
That is probably what happened to the dinosaurs.
Other animals did not die out, but went
   south, where it was warmer.
Still others stayed in the cold north.

MUSK OX

GIANT ELK

IBEX

Some of the animals which lived during the Ice Age.

Many animals of the Ice Age grew
heavy coats of hair.
The hair protected them from the cold.
The woolly mammoth was one of these.
It lived in what is now Europe,
and in China, Siberia, and Alaska.

BISON

WOOLLY MAMMOTH

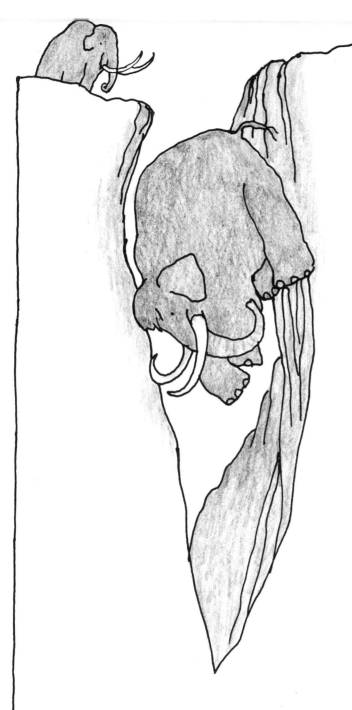

One day, a woolly mammoth
   fell into a deep crack
   in a glacier.
It broke some bones and died.
Snow and ice covered its body.
Thousands of years passed.
Slowly the weather grew warmer
   again.
The Ice Age ended.
Ice began to melt.

In 1901, the mammoth's body was discovered
   in Siberia.
Part of it was showing above the ice.
Men passing by noticed their dogs sniffing
   the rotting flesh.

Scientists uncovered the body.
Most of it was still frozen.
That part was perfectly fresh.
Dogs ate some of the meat, and liked it,
   even though it was more than 10,000 years old.

The food the mammoth had eaten before it
died was still in its stomach.
And what food!
There were about thirty pounds of flowers,
pine needles, moss, and pine cones.

Later, scientists tasted mammoth flesh, too,
and lived to brag about it.

Now scientists know a
  great deal about this
  ancient animal,
  even though the last one
  died thousands of
  years ago.
Scientists found more
  frozen woolly mammoths.
They found other kinds
  of mammoths, too.

The imperial mammoths lived 3 million years
   before the woolly mammoths.
At first the imperial mammoths were about
   the size of a pony.
But by the time of the woolly mammoths
   they had become the biggest mammoths of all.

Imperial mammoths were not hairy.
They didn't need to be.
They lived in the warmest parts of the world.
They lived in giant forests.
Their teeth were flat, like those of the woolly mammoth—
   perfect to grind and crush leaves and twigs.

The Colombian mammoth lived in a warmer climate, too.
It traveled from Asia to Europe, and to parts of America.

Sometimes it is called the
     Jeffersonian mammoth.
It was named after Thomas
     Jefferson, who was
     president when one was
     discovered in the
     United States.
President Jefferson was
     interested in the past.
He encouraged scientists to
     find out more about it.

Thomas Jefferson collected bones
of ancient animals.

Mammoths were mammals.
All mammals are warm-blooded.
They usually have hair.
They have milk to nurse their young.

Mice, bats, monkeys, bears, and whales are mammals.

So are human beings.

Mammoths were the giant land mammals of
    their time.
They roamed quietly in groups.
Mammoths were peaceful plant eaters.
They did not have to hunt other animals for food.
But they had enemies.
One was the fierce saber-toothed tiger.

There were other enemies, too.
Man was the mammoth's greatest enemy.
Inside dark, damp caves scientists found out
  how important the mammoth was to early man.
They discovered paintings of mammoths on cave walls.

They found clay figures and bone carvings
    of mammoths and other animals.
They knew no animal made them.
They were made by early people who lived
    in the caves.
They were made in the days of the mammoth
    hunters, more than 25,000 years ago.
These hunters used tools made of stone,
    so we call their time the Stone Age.

These are some of the things found in caves in France.

Woolly mammoth carved in stone

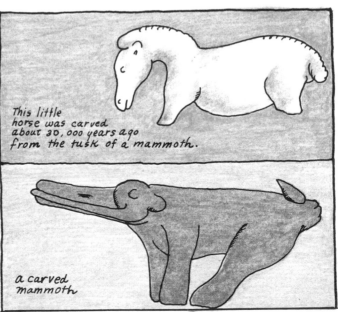

This little horse was carved about 30,000 years ago from the tusk of a mammoth.

a carved mammoth

Bone knife carved with bison and plants.

A whole Stone Age village was found in
   Czechoslovakia and dug up.
Archaeologists, who are scientists who study
   ancient ruins, learned a lot from this village and
   others like it.
They learned more about mammoth hunters and
   how they lived.
This is what they found out.
Mammoth hunters left the caves where they lived
   in the winter.
In the spring they moved to river valleys where
   herds of mammoths roamed.
They made tents in the valleys to be near the
   mammoths.

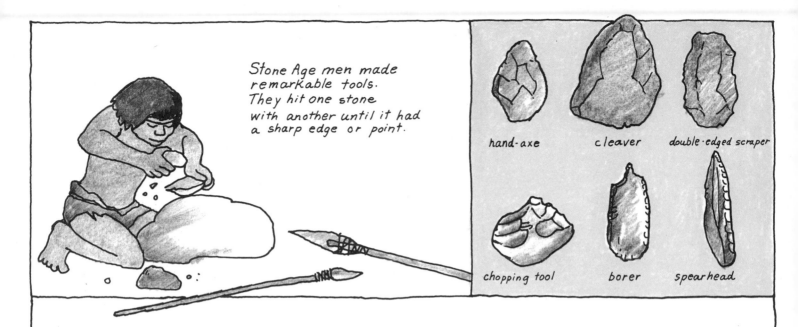

Stone Age men made remarkable tools. They hit one stone with another until it had a sharp edge or point.

hand-axe

cleaver

double-edged scraper

chopping tool

borer

spearhead

The mammoth hunters made knives and other
  tools of stone.
They used wooden spears with sharp stone points
  to kill the mammoths.
But first they had to trap them.
Sometimes the hunters made fires around the herds.
Then they forced the frightened mammoths down
  steep cliffs.
Other hunters waited at the bottom to kill the
  mammoths with their spears.

Sometimes the mammoth
hunters dug deep pits.
They covered the pits
with branches and earth.

When a mammoth
walked over the pit,
the branches broke,
and the mammoth fell in.

It could not escape.
Hunters rolled heavy stones
down on it and killed
the trapped mammoth.

Many mammoths found showed that
their bones had been broken.

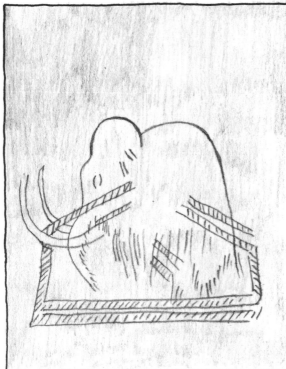

This Stone Age painting
was found on a wall
in a cave in France.

Some people think
it shows a mammoth
caught in a pit trap.

The hunters and their families ate the
    mammoth meat.
They crushed the skulls and ate the brains.

They used the bones to
make tent frames.

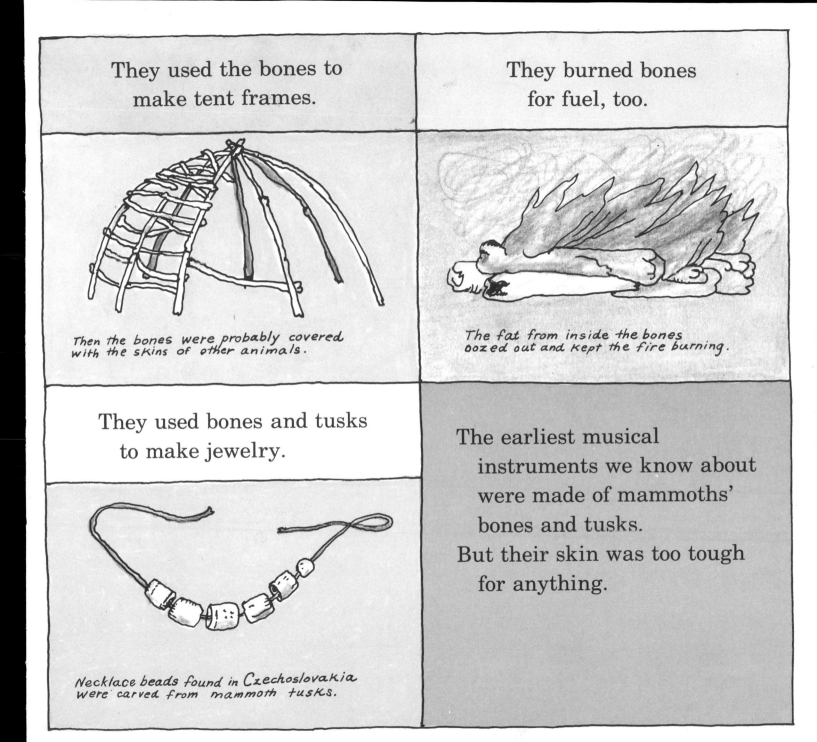

Then the bones were probably covered
with the skins of other animals.

They burned bones
for fuel, too.

The fat from inside the bones
oozed out and kept the fire burning.

They used bones and tusks
to make jewelry.

Necklace beads found in Czechoslovakia
were carved from mammoth tusks.

The earliest musical
instruments we know about
were made of mammoths'
bones and tusks.
But their skin was too tough
for anything.

These people hunted other animals, too.
The woolly rhinoceros and the giant sloth lived then.
Today they are extinct.

But bison, reindeer,

horses, and foxes,

which also lived then, have not died out.

Mammoths were hunted for a long time.
There were plenty of them, and one mammoth
   was enough to feed many families.
Today there are no mammoths.
Some people think it was the mammoth
   hunters who killed them all.
Perhaps they died out when the climate
   grew too warm.

No one knows.
But not one live woolly mammoth has
been seen for 11,000 years.

About the Author-Illustrator

Aliki Brandenberg has been interested in ancient life for a long time. This book is a result of a letter she received from a young reader, who had learned about a mammoth feast in *Fossils Tell of Long Ago* and asked, "What ever happened to the woolly mammoth?"

Aliki grew up in Philadelphia and was graduated from the Philadelphia College of Art. In winter she hibernates in New York with her family—her husband, Franz Brandenberg, also a writer of children's books, and their two children. In the summers they travel together. This year they drove through Mexico, Guatemala, and the United States. They crawled through caves where ancient people lived, and walked through lands where mammoths roamed.

7/14/93